Your Complete Guide to Risk Management and Trading Strategies

Become an Expert with Super-Easy Tips to Avoid Loss and Maximize Your Profits

Steven Moore

Table of Contents

Risk Management and Account Management

Both account and risk management exercises are activities that coincide as you go through the Day Trading investment cycle. You need to ensure that you achieve your aims of making significant profits while at the same time mitigating losses from the capital in which you invested.

Managing your account and the risks associated with Day Trading involves the responsible handling of the available equity in your brokerage account. You can perform account management through further investment in profitable stocks, ingenious trade maneuverability, or exiting from trade deals that stagnate.

On the other hand, your risk management strategies involve responding appropriately to alleviate prospective losses in an uncertain future and limiting the degree of your exposure to financial risks. The following are some of the primary strategies that you can apply to your Day Trading to ensure active risk and account management:

Hire a Stockbroker

As a beginner or a new investor participating in Day Trading, it could turn challenging if you went at it alone. You need advice on the right stock opportunities to invest in, guidelines on handling probable financial risk exposures, and technical analysis knowledge to keep track of your capital progress.

A qualified and registered stockbroker typically offers these financial services at a commission or flat fee. You need to seek such stockbrokers' assistance to tap into their experience and expertise in Day Trading. Besides, the chances of attaining your profitable goals increase when you employ the services of a stockbroker.

Account management and risk management are strategies that are innate to a stockbroker, especially when given access to the account. Therefore, you need to open a brokerage account from which all your Day Trading activities take place. Maintaining liquidity in this account is as essential as making the right trade deals.

Since you may not interact with the stock market all the time, running the trading account becomes your stockbroker's responsibility. You need to give him or her freedom to make informed choices on long and short trades, however risky they might seem at first. Trust your broker to understand what they are doing with the account and hence the need to hire an honest stockbroker, preferably from a well-known brokerage firm.

Besides, it is usual for your stockbroker to have extensive experience with managing financial risks. Most of the strategies meant to combat potential financial threats such as spreads are somewhat complex to understand, let alone apply them effectively. The same levels of complications and fair sophistication apply to the tools used for technical analyses.

You need to follow these analytic tools to make informed choices based on their data. A stockbroker comes in handy at this point to assist in data interpretation. You also get to learn about the various management strategies of which you had no idea previously. Generally, account and risk management in Day Trading is often all about making the correct technical analysis decisions.

Develop a Trading Plan

This document is a crucial tool for you as a new investor in Day Trading. If you do not possess such a program, it may be time to develop one tailor to your specific trading. Creating a trading plan is an activity that you need to perform with the help of your stockbroker. The broker typically has experience in the Day Trading sector, and so he or she can offer you pointers on the trading opportunities that have the potential of being productive. Based on this vital tip, you can create a comprehensive trading plan containing an overall objective set. Besides, the program should have tactical or short-term goals set at regular intervals during the cycle. The primary purpose of these operational targets is to enable you to keep track of the progress of your Day Trading activities.

Once you complete the creation of a trading plan, you must stick to its guidelines at all times. You and your broker need to have a chance at Day Trading's success. Hence, you both have to adhere to the rules of the trading plan. It sets out instructions on how you should react and what measures to take with your capital under different situations. Since Day Trading's future is often uncertain, it is essential for your plan to cover emergency financial responses. If you diligently adhere to your trading plan, your likelihood of attaining profitable returns eventually increases significantly. Besides, you will have a policy of intervention to potentially risky financial exposures.

Maintain Simplicity

In Day Trading, you may falsely believe that you need to overextend yourself on high-risk investments to make substantial amounts of return. This belief is a dangerous position for you to adopt when getting into Day Trading. Keep in mind that the underlying stocks are often a more volatile type of security than other investments. Fluctuations in the value of the traded stock are frequent and typically occur over a relatively short period.

You must learn how to make small trade deals on the stock from the trading spectrum's low-risk end. Beware of succumbing to the desire to stick your neck out for the riskier stocks. Greed and emotional influence are the leading causes of such irresponsible trading practices. In the case of a specific trade deal turning awful, you need to exercise restraint from the urge to make illogical trading decisions to try to cover your previous loss.

Besides, keep an eye out for volatile stocks and avoid trading in them as much as possible. If you can, distance yourself and your portfolio from such stocks. Ask your broker to let go of highly fluctuating stocks entirely due to their corresponding high levels of financial risk. All these missteps are easily avoidable when you stick to the simple trading practices laid out in your trading plan.

As a result, you will evade massive losses associated with complicated, high-risk trading subject to a high level of emotional influence. Proper and responsible account management demands that you avoid rash decisions that may lead to prospective losses and missing out on potential profits. Risk management also takes care of itself by minimizing your exposure to the high-risk end of the trading spectrum and keeping clear volatile stocks.

Establish a Stop-Loss Level

To manage the amount of risk you are willing to expose your trading portfolio, you can issue orders that reverse potentially hurtful financial positions. A stop-loss order limits the amount of stock price that you can tolerate without taking a significant financial hit.

This order enables your stockbroker to cease all the Day Trading activities immediately. It allows them to instantly stop either buying or selling any further stocks based on the unfavorable prices. The order indicates the specific stock price beyond which you canno purchasing or offloading, respectively, because doing so would expose you to an apparent financial loss.

Getting into an apparent losing situation is an irresponsible practice on your part. Eventually, you will end up with a depleted brokerage account due to the mismanagement of the available capital that you previously had. Stop-loss orders are especially useful when conducting Day Trading on volatile stocks. It is advisable to set the stop-loss order to an amount that is as close as possible to your trading entry point.

Besides, close monitoring of your particular stock's fluctuating price As you can realize when used in this manner on volatile stocks, such stop-loss orders act as risk management tools that mitigate the financial downside associated with rapidly fluctuating stocks.

Determine Your Position Size

Position sizing involves making decisions on the amount of capital to take part in a particular The size of your investment is directly proportional to the level of risk exposure. A high-volume trade will invariably expose you to more financial risks than a small number of trade deals.

Your brokerage account will often get caught in the crosshairs of high-risk transactions and Day Trading practices. Exhaustion of the amount of available capital in your trading account becomes even more likely. Therefore, an early determination of your trading position is essential before engaging in any form of transaction. Your position size divides into an account and trade risk based on the number of stock shares that you acquire on a particular trade.

For you to minimize any potential financial downfall resulting from the degree of your account risk, you must set a limit on the amount of capital to trade in each deal or transaction. A fixed ratio or small percentage is often the recommended format for this account limit. Maintaining consistency is vital in setting these account restrictions.

Do not keep altering the allocated portion for different trading deals. You should pick one value and apply it to all of your transactions during the Day Trading. A preferable limit should be one percent of your available capital balance or less. Make sure to adhere to simplicity's strategy by making only small amounts of capital allocations to the low-risk stocks.

In addition to the risks to your trading account, the other financial exposure from position sizing concerns the trade risk. The best strategy to counteract trade risk involves the use of stop-loss orders. The gap between the entry point to your Day Trading and the specific numerical amount set as the limit on the order constitutes your trade risk. As earlier mentioned, this order enables you or your stockbroker to exit from a trade deal upon

Reaching the set limit of loss. This action results in capping further loss of capital; hence, it contributes to managing financial risk in this manner.

Consequently, you should execute stop-loss orders close to your trading entry point to minimize the likelihood of potential losses spiraling out of control. Be careful not to set it excessively tight to inhibit your ability to carry out any trading. Position sizing is responsible for both account and risk management. The evasive maneuvers described usually contribute towards minimizing risk.

Remember to allow for some flexibility when setting the restriction value on a stop-loss order. You need this leeway to give your stocks a chance to increase in value without encountering an obstacle in the form of the stop-loss order. Such moves enable you to maintain a healthy trading account. As previously mentioned, the number of shares needed for a potentially profitable trade relates to your ideal position size, as shown below.

The ideal number of shares required (Position Size) = Account risk / Trade risk.

Tips for Successful Day Trading and Big Profits

Every trader wants to beat the system, to find the share that shoots up in value and makes them a fortune overnight. Unfortunately, in reality, there are very few opportunities like this. Amassing a personal fortune through the stock market is achievable, but it is usually achieved by regularly making small amounts of money and learning from the inevitable losses. Those who stick to a plan and build their funds slowly, using their initial investment and not the profits, can make exceptionally good profits and a comfortable standard of living.

To assist you in achieving the desired results, it is essential to apply the following tips to your day trading techniques:

1. Don't Trade Every Day!
This may seem like a surprising piece of advice to give to a day trader, someone who, by the very definition of the role, trades in a day! However, any type of trading is incredibly stressful. There are days when your trades will go exceptionally well, and you will feel like you are on top of the world. On other days the market has gone against you, and you will not know which way to turn.

To ensure you stay sane and have the right attitude when you approach your computer and start trading, you should not commit to trading every day. As a day trader, you should have closed all your deals out at the end of the day so, whatever the financial position, you can afford to take a day off. To be a good day trader, you need to have a healthy life/work balance; this means not being afraid to take a day off; the market will still be there the next day. Even if a great deal happens on your day off, there is no guarantee you would have spotted it in the heat of the moment.

2. Supply & Demand

The most effective way of finding the right shares to trade-in is to study the market as a whole. You need to locate the places where there are a supply and demand imbalance. More people want the shares than there are sellers, or there are more shares than buyers. These are the most likely shares to make you a profit as the market will automatically rebalance itself.

The bigger the imbalance in the availability and requirement for shares, the bigger the potential profit. If shares are plentiful and the demand is low, then their price will be low. As they get bought, they will become rarer, and this will force the demand up. The higher the demand is, the higher the price that can be charged.

These imbalances can be created very quickly and will correct themselves quickly. You need to be vigilant when surveying the markets and act quickly when you see the right criteria.

3. Price Targets

A price target is an amount that you will sell at or an amount you will buy. Your selling price is often worked out as a percentage of your buying price; this ensures you can allow for any transaction fees and still make a profit.

It is essential to set these prices as soon as you purchase any stock; you have not already decided the values before. You then need to stick to them. One of the most important elements to becoming a successful day trader is not to be too greedy. If the shares reach your pre-set target, you sell; holding on to making a little extra profit is likely to backfire and cost you a lot of money. You must be content that your calculations are correct and that you are making a profit.

4. Reward Ratio
Many traders will tell you that the reward ratio is useless. This means that they do not understand it and how to use it to improve their trading average. Used in conjunction with the other tools and good research, it can be an invaluable strategy.

In essence, the reward ratio specifies that every trade deal's reward must be three times the risk associated with the deal. This rule means that you should expect to get three dollars back for every dollar you invest and risk losing. This is an excellent ratio to adhere to when first starting; as your experience and knowledge grow, you may be comfortable reducing this ratio.

As well as using this simple calculation when deciding whether to purchase stock or not, it can be used to assist with managing your position during stock transactions and whether to sell your stock or not.

5. Discipline

It is important to remain emotionally detached from your stock purchases and act following each scenario's right business decision. This takes discipline, and it an important strategy to ensure successful trading. Failing to stick to your own rules and principles will leave you exposed to a deal for longer than you need to be and can result in huge losses when you could have made a healthy profit. The market can be very volatile, and it is important to stick to the plan you have made.

It can be very easy to watch your share prices rise and believe they will keep doing so. Instead of sticking to your business tactics, you become emotionally involved and attached to your shares; this can spell disaster! You have spent the time devising the right plan for your situation and must have the discipline to stick to your plan.

6. Losses
Even if you are the best organized and most cautious day trader in the world, you will, at times, have losses. This is an inevitable part of any kind of stock market trading. It is essential to accept this and accept any loss when it happens. Assuming you have only investment funds you can afford to lose, it is not the end of the word, and you will make money a different day.

Losses only become an issue if you make it one; you must deal with them; learn from the mistake you made, and then move on. There is no benefit in going over them again and again.

7. Budget
As already mentioned, day trading is not a get-rich-quick scheme; it takes hard work, dedication, and good planning. Before you even start trading, part of your planning stage should be to work out your budget. You will need funds available to make your first trade; you will also need to purchase a good computer or desktop; if you do not already have one. Alongside this, you will

need to download and install the right software. Many brokers will provide software when you set up a brokerage account. You need to ensure you are comfortable with their package and possibly allow funds to add additional packages such as data monitoring or an independent trading software solution.

Your budget will ensure you have enough start-up capital to purchase all the equipment you may need and start trading. There is no minimum amount required to start trading from home, although many online accounts ask for a minimum initial deposit. The more funds you have available, the more deals you can try; each one will help you understand the right approach for your personality and investment type.

8. Trading Personality

Your personality will shape the type of trading you should undertake. If you can make quick decisions and often do so, you are likely to be good at scalping. Each trade lasts only a few seconds or minutes before the next one requires a decision.

Alternatively, you may prefer to study all the facts and then base your decision on these facts and your personal experience. If you are one of these people, then you are more likely to be comfortable and good at long-term trading or possibly swing trading. These are trading styles that will allow you to think through the various angles before reacting.

As well as the ability to make quick decisions, there are a variety of other factors which will help you decide which type of trading to undertake:

- **Patience** - the less patient you are, the better you are at short-term investments.

- **Emotional Vulnerability** – If you cannot turn off your emotions, you may struggle to stick to your own trading rules.

- **Ability to be flexible** – This can be an important trait in some areas of the market

- **Passion** – The more passion you have for the subject, the better your inclinations and commitment will be. This trait is essential to being a successful trader.

9. Choose the Right Market

You need to choose the right market for your personality, time available, and even the time of day you would prefer to trade during. There are many different markets, and you can choose to day trade in all of these markets. But, when you first start day trading, it is advisable to start in one market and work your way up to two, three or even four!

Technology has made it possible to trade in any market around the world, this means that even if your preferred or only available time to trade is between midnight and six in the morning; you will trade in one of these markets. This will be one of your deciding factors. The most common markets are the stock exchange and the currency market, but the strategies this book teaches you will apply to any market.

10. Demos

Whether you choose to use the software supplied by your brokerage account or something from an independent firm, you are almost certain to be offered the chance to try the software first. It is essential to try out the software; it may be the best product globally, but if you are not comfortable finding your way around it, it will not be the right one.

The same applies to the idea of trading on the stock market. The majority of brokers will give you access to a free 'demo' software that will allow you to trade on the stock exchange without risking your money and making any money. This is an excellent way to build your knowledge of the trading markets and improve your skills.

11. Trading Plan

As with any business venture, you need a plan. The trading plan will cover your financial abilities and the markets you intend to trade-in. It will also cover your risk and how exposed you are prepared to be. A good plan should assess your current skill set to confirm you are ready to start trading; this is a physical and mental state. The plan will also help you to establish your goals and give you something to work for. This may be becoming good enough to make ten successful trades every week; it may even be having a set percentage success rate for your trades.

Whatever goals you choose to set yourself, you will need to break them down into achievable smaller goals and then work towards these goals week by week.

Part of your plan should also include making sure you have the time to research your potential investments properly.

12. Trading Journal

Your journal should be filled in daily; it should be a record of your trades, your profits and your losses. Perhaps most importantly, you should note your thoughts of possible investments and which ones performed as expected. This journal will provide you with valuable insights as you continue to trade. It will illustrate to you when you should trust your judgment and inspire confidence in your operating techniques.

It can also give you some useful information regarding how specific shares reacted in various market conditions. This type of information can be extremely beneficial as you continue and improve your day trading technique.

13. Flexibility

Once you have put your own rules into place and become accustomed to working within those rules, you will adopt a slightly more flexible attitude. This is not an excuse to say that you can ignore your own rules and chase extra profit! Adopting a flexible approach simply means that you can appreciate when a market opportunity outside of your intended scope presents itself to you and that you are not afraid to act on it.

The rules concerning risk and reward still apply, but you are not so rigid as to miss an opportunity. The longer you trade and the more experience you gain, the more you will see opportunities.

14. Analysis

One of the most important things you should do regularly to ensure you become a successful and profitable trader is to examine your trades and work out when you made the right decision. It may become apparent that there were several occasions when you made the same mistake or even the right decision. You can then study this and work out whether this decision could be applied to other market areas to achieve similar results.

Looking over your performance also helps to keep you grounded as it reminds you that not all your trades work out perfectly. It is one of the best ways of discovering your mistakes and learning from them to ensure you are a better trader in the future.

15. Confidence

Being confident is not the same as being arrogant! However, to be a successful trader, it is essential to have confidence in your abilities. You must believe that you can make the right decision and then follow it through, even if the market conditions change and it turns out to be the wrong decision.

Only by having confidence in your abilities will you make a decision quickly when you need to. If it turns out to be the wrong decision, then simply learn from your mistake and move on. Your confidence must go hand in hand with a positive mental attitude.

16. Work Place

Working from home does not mean you should not take your job seriously. You must create time every day to study the markets, review the news and possibly indulge in your trades. If you do not do your homework and stay in touch with the latest market developments, you will have an increased risk of making the wrong decision as you will not be aware of all the facts.

An essential part of working from home and taking the time to engage in all the relevant processes is having a separate space to work at; without distractions. No matter what role you perform, it is very easy to procrastinate, costing you dearly. Create a unique workspace that will ensure you are completely focused on the markets and trades, ensuring every trade is successful.

17. Educate

There are a variety of options to improve your education and knowledge of the stock market. You should choose the one that suits your personality and needs the best. You may even want to do every method going!

There may be night schools or part-time college courses near you that will help you understand how the stock market works and even provide various tips and techniques to improve your trading options. You may be able to attend seminars held by professional investors, which may improve your knowledge.

Perhaps the most important way of educating yourself and improving your stock market knowledge is to be open to learning every day. Learning can come from contact with other investors or reviewing your trading and learning from your mistakes. Provided you are open to improving your knowledge, and you will continue to learn and develop.

18. Discussions

The internet has made it possible for many people to share their experiences and even provide tips on upcoming stock movements. While you should be cautious about any tips provided by others, there is a lot of information that can be absorbed from the online forums.

You can join as many forums as you like and seek advice from others concerning specific trades or simply share experiences. A forum will help you unwind after a hard day trading with other people who understand the procedures and stresses. It can be an excellent way of learning and de-stressing before you spend time with your family or friends.

19. Consistent

Whatever approach you take and whichever markets your trade-in, it is important to be consistent. This is especially important when you are first starting investing, as you will need to know what approach you took to adjust and improve on it in future trades.

Consistency is also important as it will help you develop a successful approach and stick to that approach. If your techniques provide consistently good results, you must stick to them and continue trading in the same way. The stock market can provide consistent results if the same approach is taken every time. Find a technique that works for you and stick with it!

20. Mobility

Whatever approach you take to day trading, it is essential to remember that it is possible to access your phone or tablet information. Although the idea conditions may be in your dedicated office space, there will be times when you need to complete other tasks or even attend to family matters. During these times, it is still possible to watch your investments and adjust your position as necessary.

Of course, if you can finish trading before you have to leave your office, you will be able to enjoy your time away from your work. Being able to trade from anywhere can be a critical component to being a successful trader.

21. Curb Your Emotions

Emotional influence on Day Trading practices can turn counterproductive very fast if you are not careful. The primary emotions to look out for are self-confidence and fear. Excessive confidence can cause you to have a false sense of self-belief in your trading abilities. As a result, you may end up making illogical trading choices and decisions based on your cockiness.

You should understand that you become more prone to develop a false sense of overconfidence whenever you are on a winning streak. The successive trade deals that end up panning out give you an air of self-belief that could be subject to abuse. You get to trust your super abilities in trading and dare to engage in more risky transactions. At this point, you will experience a massive financial catastrophe, especially if you overextend yourself financially. Beware of situations that seem too good to be accurate as well.

The other emotional input of concern is the fear of experiencing losses. Overcoming this fear is possible as long as you trade in money that you can afford to lose if the transaction goes wrong. In Day Trading, you are bound to have trouble due to market fluctuations, especially when dealing with volatile stocks.

Losses are part and parcel of Day Trading, and you must learn how to bounce back after a particularly nasty run of successive losses. You may experience crippling fear that could render you unable to continue trading if you do not have a coping mechanism for potential losses. Besides, the fear of further losses may discourage you from taking risks resulting in missing potentially profitable opportunities.

Fear is responsible for holding onto a stock position for too long, as well. Instead of selling your shares at a reasonable profit, you may decide to wait on much higher prices leading to a loss if the stock price trend undergoes a reversal. Another critical factor to consider in risk and account management is the tendency to chase after quick profits to cover a recent run of bad trade deals and accompanying losses.

You must adhere to your trading plan guidelines and instructions even during such tough times. Do not modify or alter your response and come up with stupid decisions that you usually would not make. Remember that you need to start making choices based on logic to ensure responsible management of your capital. Emotional corruption can hamper your ability to make significant profits and expose you to unnecessary risks.

Find Stocks

Periodic Table of the Stock Market

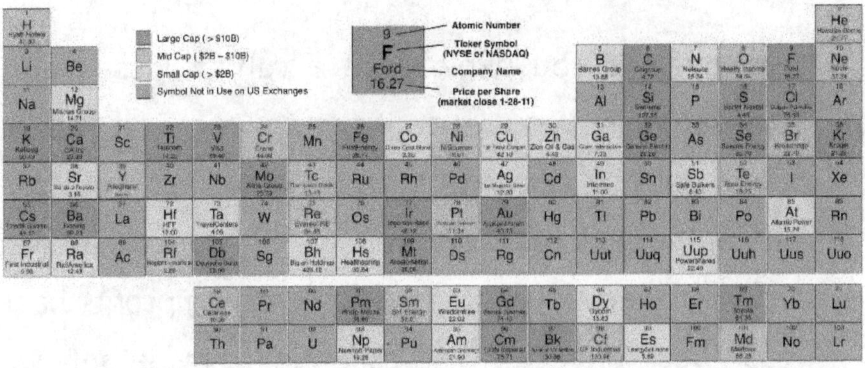

In Day Trading, you will need to deal in stocks and their fluctuations in prices. Buying and selling stocks depend on the number of shares of a particular stock that you have. When you conduct profitable trade deals, the chances are that you will have a healthy trading account. Your account's available capital is vital to enable you to continue investing in Day Trading opportunities.

However, if you experience a run of losses and bad transactions, you are likely to run out of capital eventually. A series of successive losses tend to cause an emotional reaction from most traders. Beware of trying to recoup your losses by chasing profits based on rash decisions. It is also essential to trade only with an amount of capital that you can afford to lose. Remember to adhere to your trading plan for guidance and instructions on how to respond to financial losses.

You can also apply the strategies laid out for risk management. Stock markets tend to vary in their trends over time, and hence, you are bound to go through a couple of difficulties. The most crucial aspect of this emotional roller coaster is how you react to both returns and losses. Besides, in case you want to increase your profit margin, you should know how you would acquire more stock for your trade deals.

Since the availability of securities for Day Trading may not be an issue, you should try to focus and narrow down your stock selections. Identification of potentially profitable stocks can be a challenging affair. However, there are tactics, skills, and techniques that you can apply to ensure that you invest in the most productive kind of stock.

Conduct Repeated Day Trading on the Same Stock

This tactic involves carrying out your Day Trading under the same conditions multiple times. You need to identify your most profitable stocks and focus all your trading expertise and time on only these particular stocks. This move ensures that you always get some form of returns from your investment since you already know how it usually performs. Avoid trading in many different types of securities or stocks. The selection of a few stocks whose market trends are easily understandable should be your next step. You can narrow your possibilities to around three or four stocks in which you can become an expert.

Once you have identified the relevant stocks, you must dedicate your full attention and monitoring to their market trends. When choosing your preferred stocks, make sure to select those with sufficient volume in the market. This strategy allows for the adjustment of your calculated position size. This flexibility enables you to apply for stop-loss orders with big margins to your corresponding small trading positions when dealing with volatile stock.

The opposite move is correct for a calm stock market. You will have the freedom to take an extended trading position coupled with tight margined stop-loss orders. Using this information, you will get to know the best periods to buy or sell specific stocks that would maximize your returns. The more you trade, the more you will be in a position to acquire more stock at a favorable market price. Eventually, you will end up with a lot of stock held as assets within your Day Trading portfolio.

Conduct Generalized Daily Searches for Favorable Stock

You can decide to perform your Day Trading activities in the old fashion way by looking for the volatile stocks that trend attractively. Volatile stocks are more likely to make significant movements in the course of your Day Trading. This technique requires a high degree of self-discipline to keep searching for productive stocks even during tough periods.

It is different from the repeated trading explained above. This trading exercise does not impose a recommended limit on the number of shares you can seek and does not involve Day Trading on the same stock repeatedly. As a result, you end up actively looking for favorable stocks from the vast online stock market to trade daily.

Ideally, you need to spend your time monitoring the market for the presence of big movers and trending well. Consider researching the day before. You need to find out information about the stock availability and potential for returns. This research may include looking into the institution or company. Besides, you can find out how the product performs with market consumers.

To maximize your likelihood of acquiring more stock, pay attention to relevant breaking news affecting the stock. Also, be on the lookout for the stocks that earnings are due and any new stocks flooding the market on the following day. All this information should give you an upper hand in your quest to purchase and hold more trading stocks.

Execute A Stock Screener Based on Preferential Criteria

This tool is a computer software program that looks for any available stocks upon its execution. You can search for stocks based on your customizable criteria. Ideally, you should seek a limited number of stock types that show excellent levels of volatility and raw volume. Restrict your search criteria to about three or four stocks as well. Such limitations will enable you to focus all your attention on the effective management of selected stocks and their trading accounts. A weekly stock screener search can occur for you to spend ample time trading on the stocks that meet your search criteria.

Beware of distractions from other commodities that are not on your search results. Succumbing to temptations from a seemingly attractive stock will result in a spiraling fall into your potential financial ruin. Also, note that if a particular stock maintains a regular rate of returns, do not switch stock types.

You have to keep profitable returns, as well. When run correctly with the relevant criteria, a stock screener can supply you with a range of various profitable stocks from which you can choose. Depending on the filtration criteria, the following are some examples of online stock screeners:

1. StockFetcher.com

2. ChartMill.com

3. StockRover.com

4. Finviz.com

To avoid wasting time on endless searches for the biggest movers and the best stocks, try limiting your searches to a handful of stocks. This search should ideally take place once a week, preferably over a weekend. Once you have identified your small group of favorable stocks, spend the rest of the time involved in actual Day Trading. Focus your attention on only these listed stocks for at least the whole week until your next search is due. By following this technique, you will accumulate and Day Trading in the stock you deeply understand and customize.

Tools and Platforms

People develop and adopt various tools and platforms to enhance a trader's experience while trading. Initially, a beginner may view the whole process of a transaction as being too difficult due to how complex some markets appear to be. However, with the right information, a person can receive proper guidelines to introduce them to the business and gradually propel them into expert traders. The knowledge will enable him or her to develop his or her technical and fundamental analysis that will inform his or her successful trading strategies.

Below is information that introduces a person to the tools and platforms that various traders utilize in their businesses. Moreover, there is an introduction to some trading aspects like Day Trading, technical indicators, chart types, and candlesticks. Read on to learn more.

Day Trading Tools and Services

Day Trading or intraDay Trading occurs when a trader enters a trade and holds a particular market position for a short time before exiting. A day trader opens and closes that position in a single day.

Associated with overnight risks and, instead, aims to use volatility to his or her advantage. A trader needs to have some tools and services essential to accessing and succeeding in Day Trading. They include:

1. **Electronics** – A day trader needs a computer and a phone where the laptop or desktop has enough memory to run the trading software without crashing or lagging. Additionally, they need a phone to make relevant communications to appropriate people, such as calling brokers.

2. **Direct Access Trading Brokerage** – An intraday trader should obtain the services of a suitable broker who fits his or her requirements in Day Trading. He or she needs to hire one who offers a low commission and allows for customized Day Trading software.

3. **Software** – A trader needs to research and find the Day Trading software that matches his or her needs and strategies well. He or she also should ensure that the computer is

compatible with the software and that his or her broker can access it.

4. **Trading Platform** – The intraday trader must learn about various Day Trading platforms and their features and select to use the one to fulfill their trading objectives. Besides, they should ensure that the platform matches their skills and knowledge concerning trading tools and analysis.

5. **Internet Connection** – A trader must have an excellent and stable internet connection to avoid errors due to poor accessibility. They view old data rather than the market's current prices since the unstable connectivity results in lagging and misinformation. Additionally, they can create backup internet access, such as having different internet providers for their mobile phones. In doing so, if one internet provider has issues, the trader can still access the other connection.

6. **Knowledge and Skills** – An intraday trader should continually learn and practice trading

to improve their skills. He or she can learn individually and practice via online tutorials or use an expert as a guide to perfect his or her trading skills.

Features of the Best Day Trading Platforms
A Day Trading platform is essential because it helps a trader transact efficiently and ensures minimizing risks and making profits. The following are some of the best Day Trading platforms and their features:

1. **Charles Schwab** – Provides the best premium features critical to a trader's success in the market and is the easiest to learn. It offers competitive rates and has a balance since it provides vital trading and functionality tools while lacking certain customization features.

2. **Tradespoon** – Has flexible rates and suits traders of all levels as it provides professional and widespread trading tools. It has a rich library of studies and historical information that a trader can use to gain further knowledge or customize their trading strategies.

3. **TD Ameritrade** – Offers a trader excellent trading tools and guidance to help beginners and experienced traders grow in the market. It also provides retirement resources for traders. It has expensive rates, as it is the most resourceful platform that also provides traders with the chance to develop and undertake real-time stock scans and other advanced analyses.

4. **Interactive Brokers** – It provides the best rates and best suits the high-volume traders due to its professional features like programmable order types like algorithmic types. It does not allow for research, but its tools suit the hyperactive and active traders.

5. **E-Option** – Offers the best features for advanced traders. It enables them to access sophisticated and customized tools that they can use to undertake in-depth technical analysis and trade moves.

6. **Fidelity** – Contains several tools that enable a trader to transact efficiently, such as

customized profiles, automatic identification of general patterns, chart trading, and drawing tools. It also offers competitive rates due to its practicality.

Day Trading Charts

Day Trading refers to a trader entering and exiting a market position in a single day. At the same time, charts use historical data to provide a trader with feedback regarding a market's conditions. A trader using trading charts in his or her trades receives significant additional information that helps them make appropriate Day Trading decisions. They enable them to study the past price movements and patterns that help them understand the current market and even make some predictions on particular trades.

A day trader needs to understand the various aspects of Day Trading charts: technical indicators and the different chart types. Knowledge of these two features enables him or her to possess a comprehension of vital tools that help him or her to make a profit from the trading day's volatility.

Technical Indicators

An intraday trader utilizes technical indicators to carry out technical analysis of the market. They enable him or her to look at and understand the various meanings of chart patterns. The patterns provide him or her with a visual representation of the market movements and trends in the market that allow the trader to make sound and profitable decisions. Some of the commonly utilized indicators in Day Trading include:

Simple Moving Average (SMA)

An SMA indicator uses an average that consists of the total amount of the closing prices in a given period and dividing the sum by the number of days. A day trader can make profits if they use a fast-moving average since the slower ones can cause losses if there is a reversal or end of a trend. Many traders frequently use a 10-day moving average because it does not lag and indicates the market's direction and considerable prices.

Oscillators

These refer to indicators such as the Relative Strength Index (RSI) and the Moving Average Convergence

Divergent (MACD) that reflect unclear price trends. The signals move between the upper bounds and lower ones, and the subsequent readings provide the day trader with feedback regarding the market conditions.

Volume Indicators

A volume indicator will signal to a day trader changes concerning the number of trades taking place. The trader will know when there is a considerable amount of transactions and indicate the area in the market where they occur. They can then quickly take up an appropriate position and make profitable moves in the Day Trading market.

Average True Range (ATR)

These indicators enable a day trader to evaluate the trades before entering them. As a result, they make accurate and well-informed decisions because the ATR indicator utilizes the actual price of securities to provide a precise representation of volatility.

Types of Charts Used in Day Trading

Many traders use different charts to maneuver the Day Trading markets. Each trading chart contains various features that work to provide diverse and useful information to a trader. A trader looks at the graphs and utilizes those that best suit their trading aim and strategies. The following are some popular types of charts that a trader can use to interpret and understand the market conditions.

Candlestick Charts

Candlestick charts are easy to understand and use, and they provide a trader with the most feedback by signaling where a price travels in a given period. They also enable him or her to incorporate information concerning frames of time. In this case, they can identify the highest and lowest price points, along with the last closing price in that particular period.

Candlesticks assist a trader in getting precise visual readings of the market by presenting only relevant information, such as the Heikin-Ashi chart that shows trends and reversals. Different candlestick charts also show various aspects of the market, such as time, volume, and price movements.

Some candlestick charts only use the price movements to help a day trader identify the resistance and support levels. The resistance levels indicate the highest highs of trade, whereas the support levels show the lowest lows. Renko is an example of such a candlestick chart that employs colored bricks to reflect trade trends.

When there is a downward trend, the blocks visible will be black, while white ones will be visible when an upward trend occurs. The bricks also move in terms of the price movement whereby a new white or black block appears in the following column if the price respectively moves above or below the previous one.

Other candlestick charts help a day trader find points of reversals and sets of swing highs and lows. These charts enable them to determine areas and conditions of bias in the market, making appropriate moves that give them gains. An example here is a Kagi chart that uses changes in price directions to signal reversals.

The intraday trader sets a particular reversal amount, and the price direction will shift to the opposite side once it reaches that predetermined percentage. It also indicates swings concerning high and low line signals, in that the lines become thinner as the market drops below the previous swing. Conversely, the line gets thicker as the stock increases above the prior swing.

Bar Charts

Bar charts provide a day trader with signals that are easy to read and interpret as they use color, horizontal, and vertical lines to reflect range or price in a given period. The horizontal lines show the closing and opening prices, whereas the vertical lines indicate a particular duration's price range. Additionally, traders use them along with candlestick charts to reflect the trading actions in the market.

A bar with candlesticks uses the variation between the low and high to show the trading range. The candle or wick's top represents the high state while the candle's bottom signals the low one. Moreover, the chart uses different colors on the candlestick to indicate the opening and closing prices within a period of interest. A red candle could represent the closing price at the low end of a candle and have the high end's opening price. Meanwhile, a green candle reflects its prices in reverse of the red candle.

Line Charts

Line charts indicate an intraday trader the history of prices by tracking the market's closing prices. The trader forms the lines when they link several closing costs in a given frame of time. He or she uses line charts along with other kinds of trading charts to get essential information for a successful Day Trading experience.

Charts Based on Time Frames

According to their aim or trading strategies, all the trading charts that a day trader utilizes contain time frames. The trader can use intraday charts breaking down into 2-minute, 5-minute, 15-minute, and hourly charts. Each time interval indicates the price actions of trade of interest, and he or she can use the information represented to make relevant trading decisions and moves.

Free Charts

An intraday trader can use free charts available online and offer the trader tools for technical analysis and advice, demonstrations, and chart analysis guidelines.

Different free charts provide various features such as delayed futures data, real-time data, and selection of frames of time and indicator accessibility. Furthermore, these charts enable traders to participate in various markets like the forex, futures, stock exchanges, and equity markets. FreeStockCharts and the Technician are examples of free charts that an intraday can access and utilize without spending anything.

Introduction to Candlesticks
The Japanese merchants developed candlesticks to monitor daily momentum and prices in the rice market in the 18th Century. A candlestick is a kind of chart that shows the opening, closing, high, and low prices in a particular period. As a result, it helps a trader identify the entry or exit points of a market since it signals how the investor's feelings influence the trades.

The broad section of a candlestick is the real body, a trader used to determine if a trade's closing price was lower or higher than the opening price. Additionally, they also employ colors to help them identify the state of the closing price more quickly.

The candlestick's real body is green or white when the stock closes higher and red or black when the stock closes lower. Hence, the colors help the trader quickly interpret the market conditions at a glance and make appropriate decisions without wasting time.

The candlesticks' different colors also represent the market's sentiments by indicating the outlooks of the traders. They signal if the traders have a bearish, bullish, or indecisive approach to the market. A trader then makes a judgment and takes up relevant positions in the market that provide him or her with gains.

Bullish Candlesticks

A bullish sentiment occurs when traders do a lot of purchasing because they expect an asset's price will increase in a given period. As a result, the bullish outlook will form an intense buying pressure in the market. The bullish candlesticks will have a long green or white real body to show that the stock prices closed at a higher place than the opening price. Furthermore, it helps a trader to determine significant price actions at a particular area and time if a long white candle appears at an appropriate support level of price.

If the price initially moves significantly lower after the open and then shifts to close in the high vicinity, the bullish candlestick forms a reversal pattern called a hammer. The sellers lower the prices in a trading session, resulting in intense buying pressure, which leads to the trading session ending on a higher close.

Thus, a hammer creates an uptrend, and its real body is short with a lower and longer shadow since sellers are reducing the prices. An inverted hammer indicates a reverse of the hammer candlestick since it develops in a downtrend. Other bullish candlesticks that a trader can utilize in the market include the morning star, the piercing line, the bullish engulfing pattern, and the three white soldiers.

Bearish Candlesticks

A bearish outlook refers to the situation where there is an intense pressure of selling in the trading markets. It occurs when traders carry out a lot of selling trades in a particular duration. The bearish candlesticks have a long red or black body that signifies that the stock prices closed at a lower position than the opening price. Therefore, as the day goes on, the stock price falls leading to the opening price higher than the previous day's close. It leads to the formation of a long black candlestick that does not have an upper shadow but only possesses a short lower shadow.

Traders also refer to the bearish candlesticks as the hanging man, and they utilize them to try to select a bottom or top in the market. Moreover, the patterns of a bearish candlestick tend to indicate a switch in the attitude of investors. The sentiment changes from bullish to bearish after a length of time. Examples of bearish candlesticks include the bearish harami and bearish engulfing candlesticks.

Indecision Candle

This candlestick differs from the bullish and bearish types in terms of its body shape. While the bullish and bearish candlesticks are long, the indecision candle has a small real body, in that the open price and the close price are near each other. Additionally, there are long wicks that attach to each side of the body and are equal in their lengths. The candlestick's body also lies between the low and the high, resulting in it being at the center of the entire candle range.

This candle occurs at a trend's top and bottom and can indicate to a trader about price or trend reversals if it develops at significant places on the chart after undergoing long moves. This candlestick's name comes from indecisive conduct since it signals both bullish and bearish activities. The stock closes at around the same place as the opening price because the bears and bulls were both very active in the market.

This double-price action leads to two long wicks on either side of the candle's body. Their presence and lengths indicate that the price attempted to shift both upwards and downwards in the trading session. Consequently, it signals that no one won in the market and failed to maintain higher and lower prices. The Doji candlestick is an example of an indecisive candle.

These features mentioned above provide descriptions and information concerning the various tools and platforms used in trading. A person needs to understand them to gain vital knowledge to trade in the markets successfully.

Trading Management

Day Trading Risk Management

In all trading forms, traders have a specific risk level that they may be willing to take. Since the ultimate aim of participating in any particular trade is to gain profits, your risk exposure should be as minimal as possible. In Day Trading, the risk incidence may not be as damaging to small- scale low-risk traders. However, failure to enforce risk management strategies may be financially catastrophic for large investors and companies. The following risk management strategies could be of use to new investors in Day Trading:

a. Employ stop-loss orders

b. Take favorable positions

c. Stick to your trading plan

d. Make low-risk trades

e. Seek expert assistance

1. *Stop-Loss Orders*

These orders provide a mechanism for you to minimize the extent of any potential losses. The stop-loss order mandates the trader or your stockbroker to cease a particular trade type upon meeting specific conditions instantly. Ideally, these orders indicate the range of values beyond which a given trading action becomes significantly unprofitable. It applies to both short and long trading positions. Falling prices are not ideal for stock sellers, and stock buyers frown on expensive costs.

For instance, you could set a particular limit for the range of losses that you may be willing to tolerate adequately. Beyond this limit, your damages would start affecting your bottom line significantly, hence the need for an immediate halt to the trade deal. To act as a risk management tool, you need to have your stop-loss orders in place long before taking part in Day Trading. In this manner, you will be covering a potential loss that is yet to occur instead of reacting to real-time unfavorable stock prices.

2. *Position Sizing*

Taking a favorable trading position is the essence of position sizing. Before jumping into any trade opportunity, you should acquire relevant information about that trade. This data should enable you to make the appropriate selection when choosing to take a position. Ideally, rising stock prices with the expectation of a corresponding upward trend in the price chart favor buying stocks. Hence, this Day Trading scenario warrants you to take a long position. Short positions are beneficial when the prices drop or when the trading chart shows a sustained downward trend in the stock price. Position sizing is more of an account management strategy but also applies to risk evasion techniques. If you grow accustomed to taking productive positions, your risk index decreases, and vice versa. Therefore, you should seek assistance with position sizing and take up profitable positions if the need arises.

3. _Trading Plan_

You need to keep track of the progress of your Day Trading investments. In this regard, you must stick to the guidelines set out in your trading plan. This plan provides you with instructions on how to react or respond to specific scenarios in the course of your Day Trading. These directives usually offer the best course of action in the event of most adverse financial situations. Besides, if you strictly stick to your plan initially, you will have no risk to manage later. Besides, you could seek the help of your stockbroker when drawing up a new trading plan. Make sure to capture every probable adverse eventuality and how to mitigate the risks associated with it.

Trading plans often discourage you from making decisions based on emotions, which would likely happen in the absence of a trading plan.

Day Trading often has small margins for either profits or losses. Therefore, you must learn to conduct small but assured trade deals in this strategy. It is advisable to refrain from lusting over the promises of impractically significant returns. The greed resulting from chasing quick profits over short time intervals is counterproductive to your ultimate aim. When you conduct illogical trades using large amounts of money, you will likely run out of your available capital sooner than expected. A simple trade has to be low in its risk index, small in amount, and a value you can afford to lose. Volatility and trade volume are factors that affect your type of trade, but if you stick to logic, your profits will outnumber your losses. Most financial risk exposures are the consequences of rash decisions and poor Day Trading habits. If you have challenges identifying viable trading opportunities, you could seek other seasoned traders or a stockbroker.

4. *Expert Assistance*

Whenever you engage in an unfamiliar trading practice, it is advisable to know what you are doing. The same advice applies to investors who are new to Day Trading.

Heeding to this counsel will spare you from financial ruin down the line. One way you could make use of available Day Trading expertise is by hiring a stockbroker. Trading blindly without any idea of the expectations is a risky proposition. Stockbrokers are often highly experienced traders in their own right. They know about all the potentially profitable trading opportunities and doomed trades that are bound to go bust.

Therefore, when you have a qualified and registered stockbroker by your side, you are less likely to get yourself into financially risky situations. You must predict a wrong trade deal from a mile away, but a stockbroker may be the next best option since you cannot. In addition to spotting potentially wacky trade deals, your stockbroker is typically responsible for managing your brokerage account. He or she participates in the different trading commitments and takes favorable trading positions on your behalf. As a result, the chances of making a fruitless trade decision are minimal.

Price Action in Day Trading

Price action is one of the strategies used by traders who take part in Day Trading. It relies on the movements in the price of the security under trade. Plotting the raw stock prices against the trading period on a chart is necessary, thereby showing your stock value's behavior over a specified time. Indicators that are common to other strategies play an insignificant role when using price action.

As a price action trader, you will not bother to determine the conditions affecting particular price movements in either direction. You will take the pattern at its face value because you put more credence to the stock price trends than their contributing factors. This reasoning could be an excellent time to sell your stock when the prices start rising due to its corresponding increase in value. A downward trend suggests falling prices; hence, buying the stock at favorable prices is possible.

Your entry point into Day Trading depends on potential profitability and minimal risk exposure as an investor or trader. Buying at the least reasonable price and selling at the highest stock price are the two main objectives in price action Day Trading. Besides, technical analysis comes from the price action of a particular stock over a specified period.

Deals with the ongoing, real-time stock price fluctuations. It is an instant form of Day Trading strategy without the lagging period or delays experienced in waiting for the relevant indicators.

You can modify your stock price chart to show distinct price movements in different colors. This color transition alerts you to a trading opportunity due to the obvious and easy spot of a price direction change. Once again, you will only concentrate on the upward or downward trend in the price and if that particular pattern will hold. The following concepts describe some everyday experiences attributed to price action Day Trading:

a. Price Breakouts

b. Candlestick Charts

c. Optional Indicators

d. Support and Resistance

e. Technical Analysis

1. _Price Breakouts_

A primary concept for you to understand is the Day Trading event of a breakout. It is common in almost all cases of price action trading. A breakout is a sudden jump in stock value in either direction from an extended hovering position. This spike in your stock price is readily visible on a price action chart. A breakout is an indicator that alerts you to a possible trading opportunity. However, it could also be a false breakout, in which case the prices would soon rebound in the opposite direction.

For instance, if a particular stock price keeps fluctuating between $25 and $27 for about a month, you would not think much of the security. Yet, if the stock price goes up to $29 in one day after the month, your curiosity and alertness would peak. This sudden upward spike in the stock price is the breakout. Ideally, you would assume that the price is about to keep rising and continue on this trajectory for the foreseeable future. Therefore, as a price action trader, you would take a long position on the same stock hoping for a significant profit from the increasing value. However, the breakout could turn out to be false, and the spike to $29 was only a one-day occurrence.

In this case, the rebound effect would cause the stock value to start dropping. A possible explanation could be that the upward spike caused many other price action traders to buy the stock, which led to more investors who previously held shares to sell. Based on the mechanism of economies of scale, this influx of stock security into the market causes its price to start falling. The price could decrease by a considerable margin past the initial low of $25 to the horror of the traders who took an initial buy position. If you bought plenty of shares based on the initial with the upswing in the breakout ($27 to $29), you would experience a massive loss afterward.

This uncertainty is part of price action trading characteristics, i.e., you can only know the previous behavior of a particular stock, but you cannot predict its future action. Learn to accept the possibility of losing some capital in such price action trades that do not go according to your expectations. Price action trading is akin to speculative trading. Hence, the best mentality you can have is to increase your profit margins on the good days more than your losing margins.

2. *Candlestick Charts*

Another mechanism that is useful in price action trading is the use of candlestick charts. These charts provide more information about the stock price that may help you make a more informed decision. The candlestick chart contains details such as the opening and closing prices of a specific stock; hence, you get to know the range of this value within a day. Besides, the candlestick charts show both the maximum and minimum amount of the stock in a single trading day. In this case, you can estimate the real value of the stock by averaging these particular values.

More accomplished day traders often use a combination of candlestick charts and breakouts in their price action strategies for a detailed source of information due to this additional data. They both eliminate the confusion caused by multiple interpretations of the same price action chart. You may see a downward trend and think that the stock value decreases, while another person might conclude that a turnaround or price reversal may be imminent. In the end, you both take contrasting positions on a single trade that are equally justifiable. This need for an overall complete picture enables you to develop a trading resolution based on a given stock price's whole trading status. For instance, a particular stock may show multiple drops in its intraday price while keeping with an overall upward trend on a week over week basis. As a result, such dreaded incidents as the rebounds associated with the stand-alone price action breakouts will not catch you off guard again.

3. *Optional Indicators*

In addition to candlestick charts, you may incorporate a group of specific indicators depending on your objective. However, due to lag delay, trade indicators are not essential to price action trading. In case you need them, trade indicators can easily fit on a price action chart.

Examples of such commonly applied indexes include:

• *Moving average*

This indicator enables you to pick out your particular stock's mean price movement over a specified time frame. This indicator centers on the average value of your security or commodity under trade based on that particular stock's most recent behavior in its purest form.

• *MACD indicator*

The acronym for this indicator stands for Moving Average Convergence Divergence. It depicts momentum by relating the previously mentioned moving average to a specific point on the price chart. This point indicates the price level at which you may decide to purchase stock, thereby making it subjective. Taking a particular position depends on this interaction. A possibly long trading position is considerable if the MACD indicator goes above your level or price point.

• *Stochastic Oscillator*

Just like the MACD, this indicator is descriptive of momentum, as well. Based on your trading hunch, you decide on an appropriate trend that your stock price will take. This hopeful trend will enable you to estimate the expected value in the stock price at a particular time in the future. Next, sit back and wait for the trading to reach your estimated time. Finally, use the stochastic oscillator to verify whether the current stock price and pattern at this new time match with your earlier speculated expectation.

• *RSI indicator*

This indicator suggests a market that is either overbought or oversold on a particular security or stock. This description is a measure of the strength of that specific stock within the stock market. Hence, the acronym for this indicator stands for Relative Strength Indicator. It enables you to make an informed judgment on the viability or risks of trading in a certain way and on a particular stock.

• Fibonacci Retracement

This indicator is useful for testing the level of support or resistance when subjected to the price action chart trends. You can obtain a detailed perspective of the stock market based on the patterns formed by this indicator. This information guides you on when and how to trade and on which particular stocks to trade.

• Bollinger Bands

Whenever you want to find out the usual trading price range of a particular stock, you should use this indicator. Bollinger bands

Typically show you the stock price limits beyond which breakouts occur. A brief consolidation of the stock price typically occurs within such Bollinger bands. A breached Bollinger band usually indicates a breakout, thereby requiring you to alter your taken position.

4. *Support and Resistance*

These terms describe the behavior of the price action trend. Ideally, you often encounter an oscillating pattern in an ordinary stock trading session. Some uptrends typically alternate with their corresponding downtrends. The highest point or level of the stock price that the stock can reach, as depicted by the price action chart, is the resistance. All trends past this point either hold position or reverse their direction downwards. A rise in a particular stock price often means that buying securities is the predominant trade activity.

At first, the stock market buyers outnumber the available security in circulation, leading to the increased price. The price chart, therefore, registers the uptrend. With high stock prices, investors who hold a lot of stock will take up short positions. More stockholders follow suit resulting in a stock market overflowing with that same stock. This time, the particular security outnumbers the buyers, and its price stabilizes, but if this imbalance continues, the stock prices will begin to drop. Therefore, the point at which the stock prices stop their upward trend is the resistance.

Support, on the other hand, is the exact opposite of resistance. It is the lowest price that a given stock reaches beyond which the only further direction becomes upwards. In the above scenario, the high stock prices begin to fall in a saturated market. The fall is due to the concept of economies of scale. More buyers purchase increased amounts of stock at progressively cheaper costs, hence the price action chart's downtrend. This downward direction in the price of commodities would scare any more stockholders away from selling.

Therefore, the market soon runs into a deficiency of available stock. At this stage, once again, the stock buyers outnumber the insufficient stock in circulation. The trend holds steady for a while as per the price action chart. A prolonged state of a low volume of securities in circulation triggers an increase in its price. This outcome is valid because of the more demand from buyers outnumbering the circulating stock supply. This change in the trend of the stock price signals the point of support.

5. *Technical Analysis*

Data from price action trading charts are essential for such indicators as the patterns of ascending triangles in technical analysis. These triangles are useful in predicting an imminent major breakout. This prediction is due to previous attempts at multiple minor breakouts by periods of a rising price trend. The pattern caused by these bull trends' efforts is typically indicative of a gain of momentum with each attempt. From this informative data analysis, you can expect an overall breakout shortly.

The technical analysis, trend and swing traders use price action as a data source for their indicators or tools. Concurrently, they can obtain information on the levels of resistance and support for the specific trade deals they participate in. For this data to become productive, the swing traders need to have the skills required for price action interpretation. Of more use to such external traders is the ability to derive relevant predictions of the corresponding breakouts or consolidation from the price action charts. Beware of applying technical analysis to raw price action data. For technical analysis to make sense, you need additional information such as the trading volume, market factors, and investor influence.

In the absence of accompanying technical analysis, the psychological and emotional weight might creep into your decisions. As a result, your mental faculties experience clouded judgment, thereby rendering you incapable of making logical choices. Price action trading is beneficial to small traders looking for low-risk opportunities to invest their small amounts of capital. They are usually searching for a quick profit over a brief period to suffice a single breakout event. Complex and in-depth analysis is probably more applicable in large-scale settings, for example, corporations, companies, financial institutions, and wealthy private investors. This investors' category is typically long-term and is often on the hook for massive capital loans over an extended period.

The Best Investing Strategies

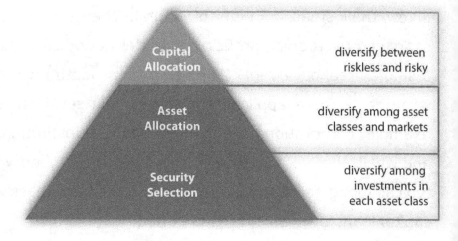

All right, you've determined what you intend to achieve with saving, so you know what sort of stocks you want. You have a grip on the potholes that can keep you up, and you learned to assess the product's success. Only one move left: to determine if all this experience is applied to your investments. It is both the simplest and the most robust move.

Think of it as a vehicle buy. You did the research: you contrasted the rates with certain distributors; you reviewed the rates of similar vehicles. We also tested the automotive selling industry to figure out whether and where this model performs well. You have spoken to former clients to see how the salesmen go about here. What's your first bid for the car? How much are you willing to consider for payments? What are the choices in the car that you want? It is time to make some serious decisions.

Rarely black and white is an investing tactic. Investment plans are typically a combination of different choices. My perception has been that my investing opportunities are rising directly as my portfolio develops. The amount of investment approaches in my portfolio is also increasing, also directly. Investment plans will stay flexible, like investment goals, adjust to the various conditions you find yourself, and adjust yourself to any fresh concepts.

A complete set of investment plans is not feasible since they are as unique as the employees. Stories talk about people who use dartboards, astrology, and (I heard) even monkeys to select their investments. For a new buyer, though, you will learn some of the more common (and healthier) strategies people use for investing in their stocks:

- Plan for the decision

- Investment approach

- Purchase and keep the dollar cost estimate. The only reaction in the field of finance is yours.

Recommendations
"Experts" tend to race from the woodworks as people hear that you have started your investing career. In all honesty, a significant amount of suggestions you get would have actual validity. Those thinking to the

Organizations with whom they operate are well-positioned than the regular citizen on the street to speak to their internal processes.

TIP 1:
A suggestion is an input or information provided from specific individuals, often not asked, that might have more insight into the product than you do.

Your friends and family will give you a real insight into a company and its goods and services that you do not know about. For starters, you asked a friend of yours who is an engineer to tell you about his encounters with the investment in the Home Depot. We're writing financial books; if it showed up and presented itself to us, we couldn't put drywall. Nonetheless, following our conversation, you feel a lot happier about my ultimate judgment.

Analysis
An analysis is an ambiguous word that may cover almost everything. To invite people to express their thoughts is to study and submit a sample of the organization's annual report. An analysis is the general public's test, as are evaluations of the stock of the Press. As an implication, it is difficult to provide a clear meaning of "analysis" for could stock and/or buyer.

This does not mean that analysis itself cannot be decided; rather, particular investors ought to decide for themselves whether "research" applies to the kinds of investment decisions they assess.

Any investment choice you make will be reviewed. The degree is up to you, but the period you can make your investment decision extremely familiar is directly linked to the investment quality. Ultimately, by betting on market analysis, you fool yourself. Don't make any mistakes; this form of cheating would cost you cold hard cash.

Purchase and keep

Purchase and sell is a great tactic for every beginner that is equally desirable to buyers of all types of expertise. Buy and keep functions such as these: since the introduction of the capital exchange. The securities sold volume has virtually, without exception, risen. The passive approach buys and keeps, operates under the premise that you can earn a profit if you acquire stock and leave it to stay where it is long enough. If it is 5, 10, or 20

Years are unclear, but knowing that your savings are part of a larger goal, you will be very confident of a return until your vision is available, and you should be able to sell your stock.

TIP 2:
Purchasing and keeping is an investing technique in which an individual buys a stock and leaves it alone. Purchasing and holding typically ensure the earnings are reinvested through future equity transactions.

For a plan for buying and retaining, you would like to buy firms' stock with a long-term opportunity. To do this, consider blue-chip inventories or inventories with strong growth prospects. Prospective owners would actively suggest reinvesting their earnings in potential equity sales rather than receiving earnings. Most companies can allow additional acquisitions without increasing inventory pressures, thus enhancing expenditure. Only the most ambitious investor is best positioned to make a return by refusing broker fees and by enabling compound interest to work its magic on the original investment or the eventual dividend reinvestments.

Finally, the most significant drawback of the buy-and-keep approach is that it needs to waste an abundance of time studying and pursuing specific projects. The buy-and-hold approach is also called the buy-and-forget regarding the policy. As a prospective buyer, you should be well informed of the size of the business. Instead of having numerous specific transactions, you're expected to do more by extensive analysis on a company and "letting it fly." The broker may dislike you because the overall trades you carry out are dependent on his or her profit, but the banker would appreciate you because you hold those trading commissions in your bank account.

The average cost of dollars
The average cost of dollars is another fantastic investing technique that needs careful consideration by new investors. In the overall dollar bill, you spend a certain sum at a daily interval; for example, you take a certain amount from a paycheck. There is little question over the best or mixed outcome of this expenditure method, and data can be found to support either view. However, the dollar's overall cost will not yield negative outcomes and places people on the table who might not spend otherwise.

One of the main reasons people offer is that they don't have sufficient spare capital to spend in the equity market. If the regular person waited for hundreds of thousands of dollars to spend before they were involved, the US equity market would be a somewhat different location. Individuals with big investments never obtain a lump sum comparable to their portfolio's total value. Instead, these large portfolios were built by making smaller investments regularly.

By the way, an average dollar price is not expected for those who want to buy to achieve better asset values. When you are curious about the amount you are charging for the product because it changes throughout the year, then you should visualize the actual amount you have charged for the product using the annual dollar cost and the actual selling price over the same duration from the following graph. In retrospect (over the previous year), you will obtain a very clear understanding of the prospects for an optimum price through buying the prospective stock utilizing the average dollar rate.

Investment Strategies And Human Behavior

The most common influence of human activity on market prices is likely to be an overreaction. All else being equal, a company's basic values on a fair market should decide the stock price, and a direct partnership will exist between the two. Nonetheless, analyses – and a quick look at CNN's inventory on every given day – indicate that the partnership will not always exist as planned.

Investors frequently respond, sometimes violently, driving rates too far or dropping them too low against their foundations. Therefore, the market is not completely justified in practice, but no financial or company-based consideration can impact. The most probable source of the phenomenon appears to be how investors view and react to shocks or news reports or even acts of specific investors. Such overreaction takes place in the financial market, which contributes to a variety of investing approaches.

Contrarian Tactics

As contrasted with existing 'favorites' or what are often considered prestige and glamor products, the overreaction impact is strongly evident. 'Out of favor' inventories are not bad-quality inventories that aren't appealing to the consumer for any reason. It is interesting, though, is that over time, the 'out of favor' stocks should usually outperform the 'favorites.' And as the "out of fashion" stocks are the "favorites" because of enhanced buying, the effect would be reversed, and the cycle continued cyclically, while only small adjustments to the market fundamental can be made. As such, commodities continue to reverse over time because consumer preferences shift, who has studied the impact of an inventory portfolio for ten years.

Primes paying for high-growth inventories are too costly when 'out-of-favor' inventories continue to show improved future profits. This reminiscent of a regression to the average, a mathematical phenomenon under which variables appear to balance and are nothing unique. Over several hundred years, scientists have understood that this form of impact also happens while human activity is involved. What is unique is that the impact was observed inside a limited stock domain.

If a commodity is an "out of favor" or its ratios, indicate a "favored stock."

In What Works on Wall Street, detailed and well-researched results were released, which include: book price (P/BV), the cash flow level (P/CF), and earnings values (P/E). Stocks with the lowest ratios will grow fastest, particularly with positive news shocks, and are therefore the ones to be pursued from this opposite viewpoint, given that they are necessarily nice stocks.

Momentum Strategies

Contrary investing approaches represent the reality that making money in stocks needs either 'out of favor' or securities, above and above the smaller yet stable returns of renowned firms like Microsoft or IBM. That is not the truth, though.

In reality, if you were to infer that theoretically, nobody should purchase through stocks-on the road to attractive stocks – and skip lucrative opportunities. However, the investment valuation requires an average of five years to make a profitable return. However, this is always inappropriate, and analysis demonstrates that the trend regularly drives a vast range of stocks to new heights and that profits can be earned on stocks even quicker than five years. You simply don't purchase securities that are up from their fair price owing to financial or behavioral factors. Such a strategy will be unmistakable and may contribute to a defeat.

The first approach refers to product combinations and utilizes the so-called large stock effect. Analysis of the returns on the investments of Andrew Lo and Craig Mackinlay on the New York Stock Exchange shows a connection the one-week return to the following, where around 10 percent of the market increase on next week's return, might be predicted from this return. Since the trend only occurs with investments, it appears that the pattern of lead/lay is seen, only with specific stocks, and mostly for the short term-i.e. regular and weekly returns. This means large stocks lead to small stocks, hence the term. Of starters, Apple rises significantly, and a few days after, there is a price change among many suppliers of computer devices.

Consequently, the purchasing of second-line stocks - medium caps and small caps - in a market that was assumed to be ready for reclassification at any point in the immediate future and then waiting on the acquisitions will operate very well. Although money may be made from trends alone, I prefer a financially stable portfolio and less susceptible to fluctuations as it travels. In other terms, you are contrary to consumer opinion, where the view of consumers is alone that such securities are inconceivable, not against basic financial determinants and economic fact.

The second approach applies to the fascinating results, which show that the high dynamic stocks – as calculated by their previous six months of income – outperform low dynamic stocks by 8 to 9 percent in the subsequent year. Therefore, purchasing high volatile stocks will be another beneficial way to maximize portfolio earnings.

They control LSV Asset Management and bring many of their work results into action. They prefer to resist preferring costly growth stocks with the momentum suffix. Instead, they use competitive indications, such as enhanced exposure and uncertainty to income reports or alerts, to disclose interest stocks that are only starting to rebound in an upward process. This is not a convenient way to shape a portfolio, time and stock choices are essential, but much like the teachers, when you have an expert programming system, you can consider it much more comfortable!

Earnings Surprise Strategies

The key to shaping a portfolio in terms of volatile stocks is to use objective metrics that show that the stock is starting that period. Also, for a particular programming system, it may be a bit tougher than it looks. When addicted to looking at stock returns over the last six months, though, profit shocks should still be seen as the driving factor of overstock collection.

One approach to measuring the benefit shock proposed by Victor Bernard and Jacob Thomas' research at Columbia University is by evaluating the shock against the assumptions of observers. When the shock is optimistic but beats the investors' standards, you are more likely to be a future winner. However, it should be recalled that what constitutes a successful, positive income surprise is not always obvious, particularly when evaluating whether income can be sustained or repeated in the future. There's no swallow in a night! Has the business ever changed?

Earnings results may often be negatively influenced by investor assessments of the industry, which contributes to overreactions in the extreme that are another valuable tactic. E.g., in three days, Intel plunged an incredibly disproportionate 20% when it announced better second-quarter incomes in 1995. Those were 4% below investor estimates, which constituted the catalyst for the decline in behavioral terms. A transition became inevitable, while profits continued to increase. During spring 1997, the market price of Intel had almost tripled. Someone who understands the organization should have made money in this case instead of joining the investing crowd.

Hewlett Packard is a common startling illustration, as it also highlights how intense investors respond to press releases. Once, the manipulation of this overreaction contributes to successful investment policy. The company announced in September 1992 that its earnings would be below the analyst's expectations. The price plunged 18 percent by the next day. It was an utterly unreasonable and excessive reaction. Truly speaking, leading to the anticipated drop in profits of a hundred million dollars in the coming year, the company's stock value collapsed by 3.5 billion dollars in 24 hours. Of note-if you have so far followed the momentum of this novel, it is not surprising to learn that the price has recovered in full in three months and then some.

With profound insight into certain forms of behavioral trading deviations, which are the product of his performance, and the perception that a successful trader should not have to gamble continually, Warren Buffet was correct to say: 'Simply glance at the market and see whether anyone has done something dumb on the day you can capitalize on.'

Fusion Policies
Another way to take advantage of overreactions that trigger price fluctuations is to take advantage of certain types of fusion situations. For example, a partnership between Royal Dutch Petroleum and Shell Transport was established in 1907. Both firms have decided to combine their responsibilities at a pace of 60-40%, but remain separate in Holland and England. Throughout the early 1990s, RDP listed mostly in the USA as a member of the S&P500 and Shell-operated in the United Kingdom as part of the FTSE100 (Financial Times Stock Exchange One Hundred Index).

While a fair economy allows for years to pass, the two business pieces will compete at the same, or equivalent, ratio of 60 to 40. Nonetheless, recent research has shown that this is not the case; company stock prices do not reflect this ratio. Alternatively, the real price differential between RDP and Shell varied by about 35% after adjusting to vat, trade costs, and foreign exchange discrepancies.

Human actions are again at work to influence and can be done with a subjective method and working with its most lucrative portion. The approach is maybe long-term, so it may be a perfect form of investing for mutual funds or hedge funds.

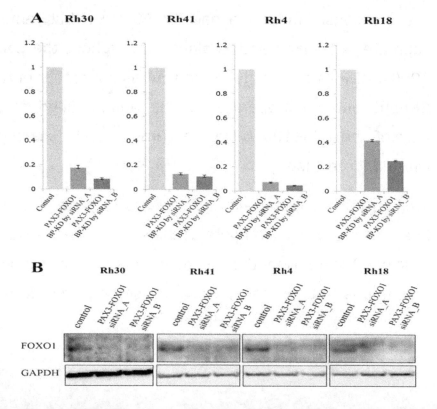

Apparent High-Risk Strategies

The clear high-risk approach involves coping with assets that are perceived to involve a rather large role because they can contribute to significant losses. This approach explains that misinformation, lack of understanding of transactions, or business conditions cause investors to assume and overreact.

Effective execution of the plan includes addressing these obstacles and evaluating the expenditure suggested rationally.

Here's one definition of junk bonds. These are high yield bonds with poor credit agency scores, i.e., BB scores or lower problems. The basic premise of this, reinforced by Mike Milken and Drexel Burnham's media reporting in the late 1980s, is that they are incredibly poor and highly dangerous. But is this assumption justified, or is it another situation where investors overreact to the details they receive rather than judge themselves? The truth is, these bonds are already available such that anyone owns them-$ 178.45 billion is reportedly sold during the five years ended in 1996 (source: Securities Data Co.). In reality, these individuals might well have based their deals on some records and studies demonstrating the good output of such bonds under the correct conditions. Notably, the low-grade bonds yield on average 50% greater than high-grade ones, and defaults were not any higher (the Hickman study on 1900-1945), the default rate was only 0.01% from 1945- 1965, and even more convincingly that even though the default rate rose between 0.015% and 0.019% by 1981, the yield premium was 4 percent.

That implied that the probability of a win was twenty times greater than the potential loss in default. Yet, there was no hope of a specific reward in the influenced thought of most investors. Despite the promise of what they think is larger returns elsewhere on the board. As Daniel Kahneman and Amos Twerski's theory of expectations suggests, buyers have remained wary of this possibility in favor of what they consider to be healthier stocks, such as the forthcoming glamorous Microsoft and Yahoo!

Junk links aren't for everybody or especially not for the beginner; to effectively exchange them, they need a strong degree of experience; they need a diversified portfolio. They need to be of decent quality, something many don't yet do. However, this approach reveals that there are several better assets than first appears on close inspection. Human nature, overreaction, overweight the interest of external knowledge such as media speculation and analyst opinion, discourage investors from seriously evaluating distressed bonds or related high-risk assets.

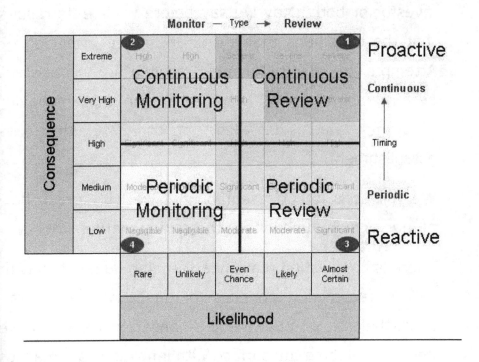

A New Generation Of Policies

Though, as we have shown, over responses may be used for various approaches, it is challenging to quantify them as a causal factor in evaluating market fluctuations. Understanding this will give us a successful plan. Nonetheless, the research council also investigates precisely what causes an overreaction. We know the impact, but what does it have? For example, is this an impact that depends on the economy or a specific investor or both? May we say before we see its results that the conditions that encourage it are in evidence? Attempts to use a formula resulted in inconsistent performance, as ABN AMRO has for their behavior program, which has lost about 27% since its establishment.

We will do a lot of research until we truly grasp how human activity functions in the capital market setting.

There is no question that understanding human behavior will increase our chances of investing in capital. Nevertheless, comportment finance specialists have begun scratching the surface with innovative approaches with a comprehensive approach to the mechanisms involved and the implementation with outcomes. In the next few years, even more successful approaches would potentially materialize. The sector itself, a beginner in the financial environment, is just around fifteen and is only starting to demonstrate interest.

CPSIA information can be obtained
at www.ICGtesting.com
Printed in the USA
BVHW041409270421
605944BV00006B/1477